Reflections

 CALIFORNIA SERIES

Vocabulary Power

Grade 4

Includes
Vocabulary Activities
Vocabulary Practice
Word Cards

 **Harcourt**
SCHOOL PUBLISHERS

Orlando   Austin   New York   San Diego   Toronto   London

Visit *The Learning Site!*
www.harcourtschool.com

ISBN 0-15-344445-2

3 4 5 6 7 8 9 10   073   14 13 12 11 10 09 08 07 06

Contents

Word Cards

© Harcourt

Introduction

The activities in this book provide additional opportunities for practicing and applying vocabulary strategies with vocabulary words students will encounter in Harcourt's social studies program. *Vocabulary Power* is divided into three distinct but related sections: Vocabulary Activities, Vocabulary Practice, and Word Cards. An explanation of each follows:

Vocabulary Activities These activities provide opportunities to review, practice, and reinforce their learning of history–social science vocabulary words and their meanings. Some activities are designed for students to complete alone; others are for pairs or groups of students. All of the activities require the use of the Word Cards.

Vocabulary Practice Vocabulary practice pages are based on previously taught vocabulary strategies. They are designed to help students in decoding, comprehending, and using new vocabulary. They include appropriate grade level vocabulary as well as a sampling of key words from the history–social science text. An answer key for this section is provided on page 125.

Word Cards The Word Cards represent all vocabulary words taught in the history–social science text, along with their glossary definitions. They can be used to study individual lesson vocabulary and to play the games in the Vocabulary Activities section. Blank word cards are included so that students can add words of their own.

Vocabulary Activities

The activities on these pages provide opportunities for students to review and reinforce social studies vocabulary words and their meanings. Two activities are designed for students to do alone. Others are for pairs of students, small groups, and large groups. All require little or no preparation and call for materials that are readily available in the classroom. You may wish to assign these to students, copy and distribute them, or place them in a learning center.

 ## Getting in Shape

Here's what you'll need: Vocabulary Word Cards; pencil; paper

Here's what to do: Choose ten Vocabulary Word Cards. For each, write or draw the word in a way that gives a hint about what it means. Use your imagination! Here is an example:

 ## Super Silly Sentences

Here's what you'll need: Vocabulary Word Cards; blank sheet of paper; scissors; pencil

Here's what to do: See how many Vocabulary Word Cards you can arrange into one very silly sentence. You'll need extra words to make your sentence complete, so cut out more cards from a blank sheet of paper and write one of the words you need on each card. Your completed sentence will be silly, but it should make some sense. You'll be a Superior Silly Sentence Shaper!

 ## Word Scramble

Here's what you'll need: Vocabulary Word Cards; paper and pencil for each player

Here's what to do: Each player should choose six words from the Vocabulary Word Cards and write them on paper, scrambling the letters of each word. Then exchange papers and unscramble the other player's words.

Sand City

Here's what you'll need: one set of Vocabulary Word Cards; scissors and one copy of this page for each player (or a blank sheet of paper and a pencil for each player for tracing)

Here's what to do: Cut out each sand castle part (or trace the parts onto a blank sheet of paper and then cut them out). Stack the Vocabulary Word Cards with the words facing up. Take the top card and tell the other player the word's definition. If you are correct, choose one of your sand castle parts and place it on the table. Then it's the other player's turn to take a card, give the word's definition, and begin building a sand castle. If your definition isn't correct, it's the other player's turn and you don't get to place a part on your castle. Keep on taking turns and adding pieces to your sand castles until your castles are complete.

Outsider

Here's what you'll need: For each player: a set of Vocabulary Word Cards; pencil; paper

Here's what to do: Sit where you and the other player can't see each other's paper. Choose four words from your Vocabulary Word Cards that have something in common. Then find a vocabulary word that doesn't belong with the others. Write all five words in a list on your paper. Repeat this four more times so that you have five lists. Write the "outsider" words, the ones that don't belong in the category, in different places in the lists so they won't be easy to find. When you and the other player are ready, exchange papers. Challenge each other to find the word in each list that doesn't belong.

Syllable Stomp

Here's what you'll need: one set of Vocabulary Word Cards, mixed up and placed in a bag

Here's what to do: In this game, you'll guess a secret word by using its meaning and the number of its syllables as clues. Reach into the bag and take out a card. Silently read the word, but don't let the other player see. Now read the word's definition aloud, and tap your foot on the floor one time for each syllable in the word. Ask the other player to guess what the word is. Right or wrong, it's the other player's turn to take out a card and give the clues. Take turns until the word bag is empty.

chan nel

 ## Ask Ten

Here's what you'll need: one set of Vocabulary Word Cards, mixed up and placed in a bag; scrap paper; pencil

Here's what to do: Players should take turns drawing one Vocabulary Word Card each until 20 cards have been drawn. One player writes the 20 words on scrap paper and places the paper where both players can see it. Now players take turns choosing a word from the list for the other player to guess. The player who is guessing may ask 10 questions, one at a time, about the word, and each question must have a *yes* or *no* answer. These are some possible questions:

Does the word begin with a consonant?

Does the word have more than one syllable?

Does the word name a place?

Does the word have something to do with water?

Whether the questioner figures out the word or not, after 10 questions it's the other player's turn to choose a word and answer the questions.

On the Road

Here's what you'll need: a large map of your state; six sticky notes; pencil; a coin or other game piece for each player; one set of Vocabulary Word Cards, mixed up and placed in a bag

Here's what to do: First, turn your map into a game board. Here's how: Working together, choose a city near the western or northern border of your state to be the beginning point of your road trip. Choose a city near the eastern or southern border of the state for the end point. Now choose four cities in between. Write the name of one of the cities on each of the sticky notes and place each note on that city on the map. Number the notes from 1 to 6, with 1 on the beginning city and 6 on the ending city, and the others in the order you would pass through them if you were traveling across the state.

Now begin the game. Place both game pieces on City #1. Player A draws a Vocabulary Word Card and reads the definition aloud. If Player B gives the correct word that matches the definition, then Player B moves his or her game piece to City #2. Right or wrong, it's now the other player's turn. Continue until both players have completed the road trip across the state.

Rhyme or Reason

Here's what you'll need: one set of Vocabulary Word Cards, mixed up and placed in a bag

Here's what to do: Divide the players into Team 1 and Team 2. A player from Team 1 reaches into the bag and, without looking, takes out a card. All the players on Team 1 should look at the word and definition on the card, but Team 2 must not see it. Now Team 2 must guess the word on the card, using clues from Team 1. Here's how:

Team 1 asks, "Rhyme or Reason?" The players on Team 2 decide as a group what kind of clue they want. If they choose Rhyme, Team 1 must say a word that rhymes with the secret word. If they choose Reason, Team 1 must give a fact about the word's meaning. For example, if the secret word is *erosion*, a Rhyme clue might be *explosion* and a Reason clue might be *Wind can cause it*. Team 2 may ask for three clues, choosing a Rhyme or a Reason clue each time, and taking a guess after each clue. Award 3 points for a correct answer after only one clue, 2 points for a correct answer after 2 clues, and 1 point for a correct answer after 3 clues. After three guesses, it's Team 2's turn to draw a Vocabulary Word Card from the bag and Team 1's turn to try to guess the secret word. After each team takes 5 turns, see which one has earned more points.

In Today's News . . .

Here's what you'll need: For each player: one set of Vocabulary Word Cards; paper; pencil

Here's what to do: You'll do the first part of this game alone. Spread the Vocabulary Word Cards where you can see the words. Now imagine you're a television news reporter, and it's your job to report on some event for the evening news. It can be something that really happened, or you can make up an event. Write your news story, working in as many words from the word cards as you can. When everyone has finished writing, get the group together and take turns reading your stories aloud. You get one point for each vocabulary word you use. After all the players have read their stories, tally the points and see who used the most vocabulary words.

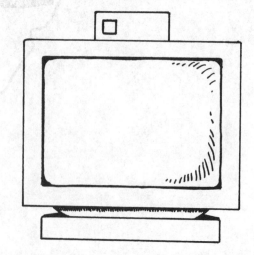

© Harcourt

Strange Stuff for Sale

Here's what you'll need: a blank sheet of paper for each player; a pencil or crayons for each player; Vocabulary Word Cards; dictionary and/or thesaurus

Here's what to do: Working alone, look through the Vocabulary Word Cards and choose one that names a place or thing. Your job is to make a poster (on a blank sheet of paper) advertising that place or thing for sale. Here's the rule: You must include a three-word description of what you're selling, and all of the words must begin with the same sound as the item that's for sale. For example:

FOR SALE!
PERFECTLY PEACEFUL,
PRETTY
PRECIPITATION

Don't worry if you've scribbled a somewhat silly sign.

When all the players have finished making their posters, show and read yours to the group. Then ask another player to give your word's definition. Take turns showing your posters until everyone has had a turn.

Decorate the Package

Here's what you'll need: a sheet of paper and crayons or colored markers for each player; one set of Vocabulary Word Cards mixed up and placed in a bag

Here's what to do: Imagine that your sheet of paper is a wrapped package that you are going to decorate. One person is chosen to be the Question Master. That person draws a word card, reads the definition aloud, and asks, "What is this?" The other players raise their hands if they know what word matches the definition. The Question Master calls on the first player to raise his or her hand. If that player gives the correct answer, he or she may draw one item of decoration (such as a bow or a flower) on his or her package. If the answer is incorrect, the Question Master reads the definition again and calls on the first player to raise his or her hand. Keep playing until everyone has a well-decorated package.

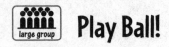

Here's what you'll need: one set of Vocabulary Word Cards; a large area where the players can move around; 4 books or other objects to use as home plate and bases

Here's what to do: Divide the players into two teams. Set up a baseball infield by placing the four books or other items several steps apart in the shape of a diamond.

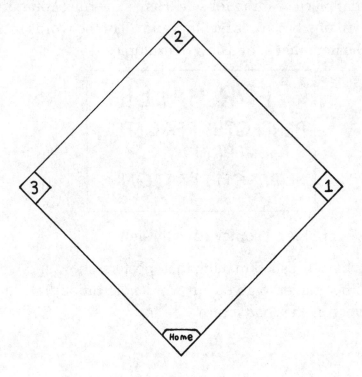

Place the Vocabulary Word Cards in a stack with the words facing up.

Decide which team will bat first. The first player from the team that's at bat stands at home plate. The first player from the other team takes the top card from the stack of Vocabulary Word Cards and reads the word aloud. The player at bat gives the definition of the word. If the definition is correct, the player moves to first base. If the definition is not correct, the player is out. Then the next player from the at-bat team comes to home plate and gives the definition of the word on the next card that is drawn. If the definition is correct, that player moves to first base and the player on first base advances to second base.

Continue the game, with the players on base advancing with each correct definition. Each time a player crosses home plate, one run is counted. When the at-bat team makes three outs or scores three runs, it's the other team's turn to bat. An inning is completed when each team has finished one turn at bat.

If you don't have time to play nine innings, ask your teacher to decide how many innings the game should last.

Match This!

Here's what you'll need: *Match This!* cards

Here's what to do: Before game time, the teacher or another person must make the *Match This!* cards. Here's how: Find out how many students will be playing the game. That's the number of blank cards or slips of paper you'll need. Write a vocabulary word on half the cards. Write the matching definitions on the other cards. Now let the game begin!

Divide the players into two groups, the *Words* and the *Definitions.* Give a word card to each member of the *Words* and a definition card to each member of the *Definitions.* Now players should move around the room and find the person who has the matching card. When all the *Words* and *Definitions* are matched, each pair should read the cards aloud.

Photo Shoot

Here's what you'll need: One set of Vocabulary Word Cards (only the nouns), mixed up and placed in a bag

Here's what to do: Each player draws a card from the bag without looking. Now read your word card silently, but don't let the other players see it. Imagine that you are a professional photographer and you have taken a picture of what's named on your card. Take turns with the rest of the players standing in front of the group and describing your photo. For example, if you draw the card *floodplain*, you might say something like this:

> *My photo shows land that is low and flat. A river runs through the center of the picture.*

Then ask the rest of the group to guess what your picture shows.

© Harcourt

Alligator Alley

Here's what you'll need: one set of Vocabulary Word Cards, mixed up and placed in a bag; two boxes to serve as alligators (If you like, you can decorate the boxes to look a little like hungry gators.)

Here's what to do: The alligators are hungry. Let's feed them! First, divide the players into two teams. Each team has one of the alligators. The first player from Team A draws a word card and reads the definition. If the first player from Team B correctly states the word that fits the definition, then that player takes the card from the player who drew it and feeds his or her team's own alligator by tossing the card into the gator's mouth. If the answer isn't correct, the card goes back into the bag. Right or wrong, it's the other team's turn. After every player on each team has had a turn, see which team's alligator has gobbled up more food!

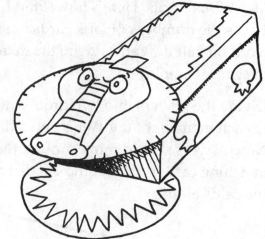

Lot-O-Letters

Here's what you'll need: chalkboard; chalk; Vocabulary Word Cards; 26 slips of paper with a different letter of the alphabet written on each, mixed up and placed in a bag

Here's what to do: One person, the Word Weaver, goes to the board and chooses a word card. Be sure that no one else sees the card, because the object of the game is to guess the word. The Word Weaver draws a short line on the chalkboard for each letter of the word. Now the bag containing the letters is passed to the first player, who draws a letter and asks the Word Weaver whether that letter appears in the secret word. If it does, the Word Weaver writes the letter on the line or lines where it belongs in the word. Whether the letter appears in the word or not, the bag is then passed to the next player, who draws another letter, and so on. The first person to guess the secret word and give its definition becomes the next Word Weaver, who chooses a different word and continues the game.

Spelunker's Adventure

Here's what you'll need: *Spelunker's Adventure* game board on pages 12–13; a game piece for each player; 8 slips of paper with the number *1* written on two of them, *2* on two of them, *3* on two of them, and *4* on two of them; one set of Vocabulary Word Cards; 2 paper bags

Here's what to do: Players of this game are spelunkers, people whose hobby is exploring caves. The object of the game is to be the first to explore the cave from the entrance to the exit.

First, mix up the numbered slips of paper and place them in one of the bags (the *Number Bag*). Mix up the Vocabulary Word Cards and place them in the other bag (the *Word Bag*). Place all the game pieces on *Entrance*. Then decide who has the first turn.

If you're first, draw a number from the Number Bag. That's the number of spaces on the game board you will move your game piece if you give a correct answer. Then draw a card from the Word Bag. Without looking at the card, hand it to another player, who will read the definition aloud. If you correctly give the word that fits the definition, then move your game piece the number of spaces on the paper you drew from the Number Bag. Then it's the next player's turn. If your answer isn't correct, you don't move your game piece, and it's the next player's turn. Either way, return the number to the Number Bag and put the word card in a separate stack.

Keep on taking turns drawing numbers and words and advancing around the game board. If you run out of cards in the Word Bag, put the cards back in and use them again. The Chief Spelunker is the first player to land exactly on the *Exit* space.

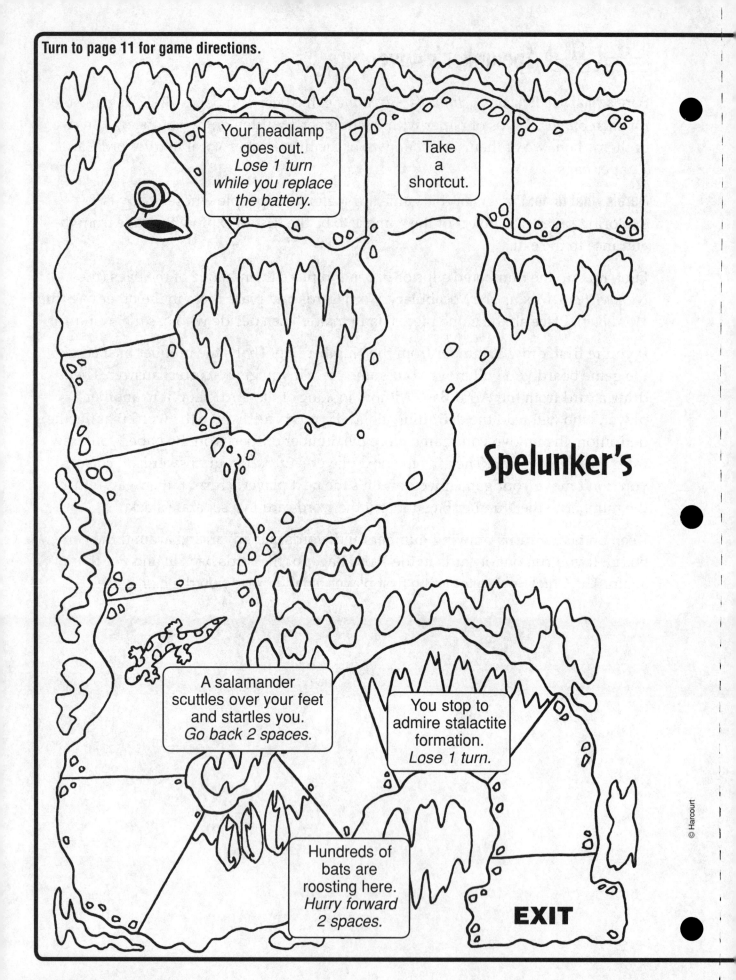

Your headlamp goes out. *Lose 1 turn while you replace the battery.*

Take a shortcut.

Spelunker's

A salamander scuttles over your feet and startles you. *Go back 2 spaces.*

You stop to admire stalactite formation. *Lose 1 turn.*

Hundreds of bats are roosting here. *Hurry forward 2 spaces.*

EXIT

© Harcourt

Adventure

ENTRANCE

Underground pool. *Lose 1 turn while you put on diving gear.*

You discover paintings on the cave walls. *Take 1 extra turn.*

Take a shortcut.

Huge stalagmites block your way. *Go back 3 spaces.*

© Harcourt

Antonyms 1

Antonyms are words that have opposite, or nearly opposite, meanings. For some words, an antonym can be formed by adding a prefix.

un- means "not"   *non-* means "not"

DIRECTIONS Add a prefix to each word below to form its antonym.

1 _____ + fiction = _____

2 _____ + realistic = _____

3 _____ + natural = _____

4 _____ + flammable = _____

DIRECTIONS For each word pair, draw pictures to illustrate the differences between the antonyms. For example, draw the covers and create titles for a fiction book and a nonfiction book.

5 fiction   nonfiction

6 noisy   quiet

7 addition   subtraction

8 alone   together

Antonyms 2

Antonyms are words that have opposite, or nearly opposite, meanings.

DIRECTIONS Read the words in the box. Then use the clues below to find pairs of antonyms. Write each word after its clue.

amateur	benefit	dabbler	disadvantage	energy	expert	exports
fatigue	imports	trainer	professional	rookie	veteran	trainee

1. someone who is paid _____

   someone who is unpaid _____

2. a feeling of weakness or exhaustion _____

   a feeling of vigor or power _____

3. someone who enjoys a task
   but doesn't take it seriously _____

   someone who studies carefully and
   has a lot of knowledge about a topic _____

4. goods sold to people in other countries _____

   goods brought in from another country to be sold here _____

5. someone who has spent many years in this job _____

   someone in the first year at this job _____

6. something that is helpful _____

   something that is unfavorable _____

7. someone learning how to do a job _____

   someone teaching someone how to do a job _____

Compound Words

A compound word is two words joined together to form a new word. A compound word may be written as one word, as two words, or as a hyphenated word.

DIRECTIONS Read each compound word in Column A. Use the beginning of that compound word to write a new compound word in Column B.

Examples:

Column A		Column B
freeway		free<u>form</u>
city manager		city <u>hall</u>
1 armchair	arm	_____
2 downtown	down	_____
3 skyscraper	sky	_____
4 watercolor	water	_____
5 self-sufficient	self	_____
6 footlights	foot	_____
7 land grant	land	_____
8 tablespoon	table	_____
9 doorway	door	_____
10 playpen	play	_____
11 toothache	tooth	_____
12 overpass	over	_____
13 undersea	under	_____
14 superhighway	super	_____
15 anytime	any	_____
16 springboard	spring	_____

Content-Area Words 1

The words in the box are all related to history.

DIRECTIONS **Use the words to answer the following questions.**

heritage	legacy	inheritance	ancestor
history	heredity	genealogy	origin

1 What word names a relative who lived long ago? _____

2 Which three words are related to the Latin root *heres*, which means "heir"?

_____

_____

_____

3 Which word means "the study of one's family history"? _____

4 Which word means "the beginning"? _____

5 Which word means "the study of the past"? _____

6 Which words mean "something handed down from previous generations"?

_____

_____

7 Which word means the opposite of *descendant*? _____

DIRECTIONS **Think about the meanings of the two words below. Write each word next to its definition.**

genealogy   history

8 a study that includes stories about
what people were like and what they did _____

9 a record of names, dates, and
places of birth, marriage, and death _____

Content-Area Words 2

The words in the box are all related to the study of oceans.

DIRECTIONS **Use the words to answer the following questions.**

marine	nautical	maritime	naval
mariner	oceanic	coastal	submarine

1 Which words are related to the sea or ocean?

_____   _____

_____   _____

_____   _____

_____

2 Which word has to do with the land? _____

3 Which words are related to the Latin root *mare*, which means "sea"?

_____   _____

_____   _____

4 Which words come from the Latin root *navis* and the Greek root *naus*, which both mean "ship"?

_____   _____

5 Which word names a boat that can travel under water? _____

6 Which word names a sailor, or person who navigates a ship?

_____

7 Which words could be used in relation to the armed forces?

_____   _____

_____

8 Which word is related to navigate? _____

Write another word from the same family. _____

Content-Area Words 3

The words in the box are all related to water.

DIRECTIONS Use the words to answer the following questions.

irrigate	trough	canal	moisten
aqueduct	hydrate	sluice	drench

1 Which four words are synonyms for "to water"?

_____   _____

_____   _____

2 Which would you do regularly, as on a farm? _____

3 Which would you do if the soil were just slightly dry? _____

4 Which would you need to do if the soil were extremely dry?

_____

5 Which four words name ways to hold or carry water?

_____   _____

_____   _____

6 Which one has a gate to control the flow of the water? _____

7 Which one can be small enough to bring water
to fields, or large enough for ships to sail on? _____

8 Write your own words related to water. _____

_____   _____

_____   _____

_____   _____

Content-Area Words 4

The words in the box name different topics or areas of study.

DIRECTIONS Match each list of special vocabulary words with one of the topics named in the box. Write the name of that topic on the line.

drama	grammar	anatomy	music	social studies

1. skeleton, muscles, veins _____

2. actors, stage, costumes, plot _____

3. nations, states, capitals, communities _____

4. sonata, piano, treble clef _____

5. subject, predicate, sentence _____

architecture	language arts	art	sports	mathematics

6. subtraction, multiplication, division, patterns _____

7. paints, brushes, easels, images _____

8. football, basketball, soccer, score _____

9. framework, structure, base, foundation _____

10. speaking, listening, writing _____

DIRECTIONS Choose two topic names from either of the boxes above. List at least four additional words related to each of the topics you chose.

Topic: _____   Topic: _____

_____   _____

_____   _____

_____   _____

_____   _____

Content-Area Words 5

DIRECTIONS Read the words in the box. Then answer the questions below.

civilization	arts	language	culture
cuisine	society	folklore	ethnicity

1 Which four words describe people as a group?

_____   _____

_____   _____

2 Which word is a label for the following: jazz, pantomime, cinema, sculpture?

_____

Give another example that fits this category. _____

3 Which word deals with the way people communicate? _____

Name two or three other words that belong in this group.

_____   _____

_____

4 Legends, myths, and tall tales are examples of _____.

Give another example of this. _____

5 The foods people eat and the manner in which they are prepared are

related to _____.

Name some dishes from a particular culture. _____

_____   _____

Content-Area Words 8

The words in the box are all related to rivers.

DIRECTIONS Write each word above the correct definition in the web.

| delta | inlet | meander | valley | oasis | tidal | tributary | source |

_____

a low point between hills or mountains

_____

a stream that feeds into a larger stream or river

_____

the beginning point

_____

to follow a winding course

river

_____

a fertile area in a desert, often along a riverbank

_____

the flat area of land at the mouth of a river

_____

a narrow strip of water leading into land from the ocean

_____

having to do with the ocean tides

© Harcourt

Content-Area Words 9

The words in the box are all related to art.

DIRECTIONS Write each word in the correct part of the diagram. Then add at least one word of your own to each part of the diagram.

subject   easel   landscape   acrylic   canvas   bristle   impression   palette

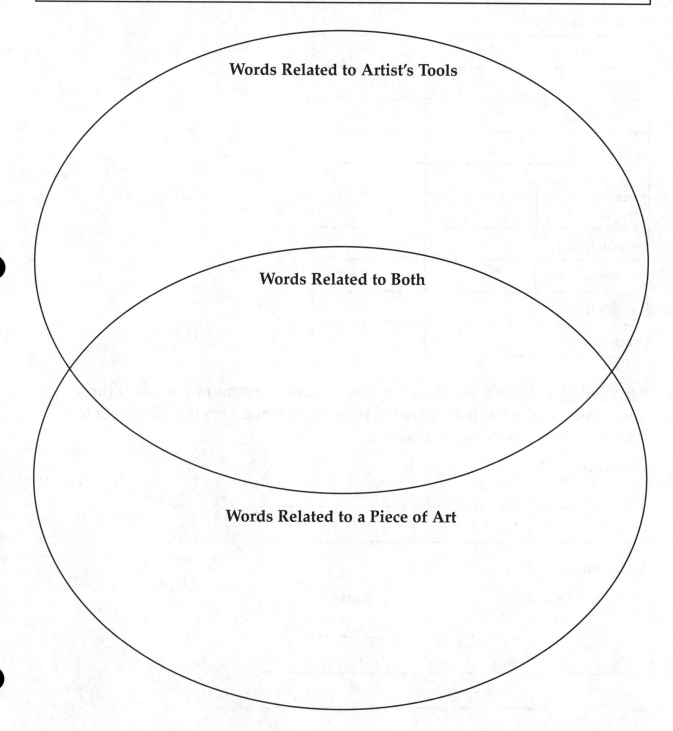

Words Related to Artist's Tools

Words Related to Both

Words Related to a Piece of Art

Content-Area Words 10

DIRECTIONS Describe urban and rural communities by checking each box that applies. Remember that rural areas also have small towns.

	Urban	Rural
boulevard		
lane		
skyscraper		
ranch		
downtown		
city center		
subway		
civic		
municipal		
metropolitan		
agriculture		
commerce		

DIRECTIONS Make a list showing how an urban community is like a rural community. Make two lists showing their differences. Use the information from the chart you completed above.

Likenesses

_____   _____

_____   _____

Differences

　　　Urban　　　　　　　　　Rural

_____   _____

_____   _____

_____   _____

Content-Area Words 11

DIRECTIONS Read the words in each group and think about how they are related. Cross out the word that does not belong. Then write a name for the category of related words.

1 diary   journal   memoir   news story   _____

2 haiku   sonnet   novel   limerick   _____

3 keyboard   magazine   memory   monitor   _____

4 textbook   novel   magazine   movie   _____

5 computer   paper   pencil   pen   _____

6 envelope   stamp   stationery   reply   _____

7 reader   author   publisher   editor   _____

8 jacket   plot   spine   pages   _____

Content-Area Words 12

All the words in the box are related to oceans.

DIRECTIONS Write each word in the correct part of the web.

dunes	Atlantic	minerals	lobsters	oil	Pacific
bay	beach	Arctic	oysters	seaweed	gas

Marine Resources

_____

_____

_____

Coastal Features

_____

_____

_____

Culture

Names

_____

_____

_____

Marine Life

_____

_____

_____

Content-Area Words 13

DIRECTIONS Read the words in the box. Use the words to answer the
question and complete the definitions below.

| fable | fiction | literature | poetry | myth | nonfiction | narrative | folktale |

1 Which word is a label for all the others? _____

DIRECTIONS Now write the word that is a label for the following features.

2 has animals who behave like humans; teaches a lesson _____

3 true stories or facts about real life; purpose may be to inform

_____

4 a story that was first told orally; is passed down and often retold

in slightly different ways _____

5 did not really happen, but may seem realistic; may be fantasy;

usually for entertainment _____

6 may have rhythm and rhyme; uses figurative language to create images

_____

7 uses story structure; may be about an actual event _____

8 fictional story from long ago; tries to explain why things are the way they are

_____

DIRECTIONS Now try this. Write the title of a piece of literature and choose
the word from the box above that labels it.

Title _____

Genre or Label _____

© Harcourt

Name _____ Date _____

Content-Area Words 14

DIRECTIONS Read the words in the box. Write one of the words to label each part of the drawing below.

pedestal	plaque	monument	dedication

1 _____

2 _____

3 _____

4 _____

DIRECTIONS Read the words in the box below. Use the words to complete the sentences. Then follow the directions in 6 and 7.

scaffold	sculpt	pedestrian

5 An artist hired to _____ a statue is called a sculptor.

6 The statue needs to be restored. On the left side, draw a

_____ for the maintenance crew to climb onto.

7 The statue is in the town square. Draw a _____ walking by.

Content-Area Words 15

DIRECTIONS Read the words in the box. Write each word after the correct clue or definition.

auditory	nocturnal	perception	extra-sensitive
ocular	olfactory	diurnal	extraordinary

1 labels for senses _____

_____   _____

2 labels for time _____   _____

3 means "out of the ordinary" _____

4 means "unusually sensitive" _____

5 synonym for *sense* _____

DIRECTIONS Choose a word from the box above to complete each sentence.

6 *Audible* means "can be heard." The _____ sense is related to the ears.

7 *Oculist* is a synonym for *optometrist.* The _____ sense is related to the eyes.

8 *Olfaction* is the sense of smell. The _____ sense is related to the nose.

Content-Area Words 16

All the words in the box are related to erosion.

DIRECTIONS **Write each word in the correct part of the web.**

| barren   abrasion   wear   gravel   windswept   glacier   weather   coastline |

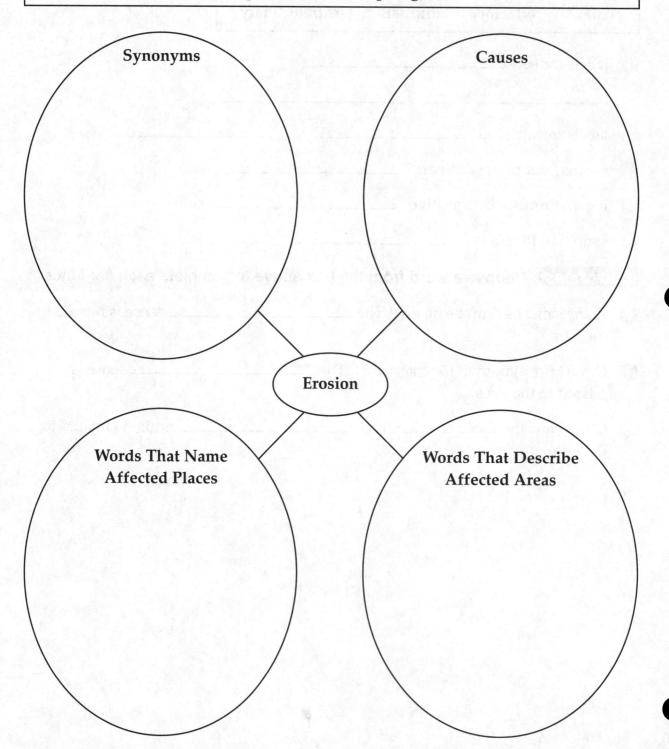

Synonyms

Causes

Erosion

Words That Name
Affected Places

Words That Describe
Affected Areas

Context Clues 1

DIRECTIONS Read each sentence or pair of sentences. Use context clues to figure out the meaning of the underlined word. Circle the letter of the correct meaning.

1 Jim learned how to manage his business's income.

   A customers and suppliers

   B phone number and address

   C money earned by a business

   D largest size of a product

2 Natural resources such as oil and timber should be used carefully.

   A forests

   B merchandise

   C supplies

   D gasoline

3 I worked out a budget so that I can buy a new bike.

   A an exercise plan

   B a method of getting something finished

   C a savings account

   D a plan for saving and spending

4 Telephones and e-mail are methods of communicating quickly.

   A transporting goods

   B sharing information

   C cutting the amount of time

   D following directions

5 Karen and Kyle went into business together. They opened a pizza parlor.

   A a venture to earn a living

   B no one else's concern

   C an errand

   D a difficult task

Context Clues 2

DIRECTIONS Read each sentence or pair of sentences. Use context clues to figure out the meaning of the underlined word. Circle the letter of the correct meaning.

1 Vitamins are <u>essential</u> to good health. They give you energy and keep you from getting sick.

   A of great importance   **C** harmful

   B possibly helpful   **D** of little importance

2 A medical test can show if you are vitamin-<u>deficient</u>. If you are, you may need to eat a lot of foods that are rich in vitamins.

   A capable of doing a good job   **C** lacking the necessary amount

   B not easily achieved   **D** put off until a later date

3 In addition to eating a healthful, balanced diet, some people also take a vitamin <u>supplement</u>. This gives them an extra dose of important vitamins.

   A a kind of geometric angle   **C** something good you say

   B something in addition to   **D** soft and bendable

4 Increased energy, or <u>vigor</u>, is the result of maintaining a balanced diet and following a program of regular exercise.

   A a feeling of weakness   **C** electric current

   B bodily strength   **D** a type of exercise

5 After hiking for many hours, we swam in the cool lake and rested in the shade. We soon felt <u>revitalized</u> and ready to head back to camp.

   A of importance to good health   **C** drained of energy; extremely tired

   B ready to go to sleep   **D** renewed in energy or liveliness

Context Clues 3

DIRECTIONS Read each sentence and think about the meaning of the underlined word. Then write a definition of the underlined word.

1 We went to the arboretum to see the rare trees and shrubs.

Arboretum means _____.

2 In botany class, we studied different plants.

Botany means _____.

3 The botanist carefully studies the leaves and roots of the plant.

Botanist means _____.

4 Oaks, pines, and many smaller plants make up the flora of our area.

Flora means _____.

5 The warm greenhouse had a variety of delicate tropical plants.

Greenhouse means _____.

6 The farmer grew flowers and vegetables in her garden.

Garden means _____.

7 The cows grazed in the lush valley, as there was little vegetation on the barren hillsides.

Vegetation means _____.

8 The botanical setting had many flowers and trees.

Botanical means _____.

9 When the rosebushes bloom, they will produce beautiful red flowers.

Bloom means _____.

Context Clues 4

DIRECTIONS Read each sentence or pair of sentences. Think about
the meaning of the underlined word. Then write a definition of the
underlined word.

1 The <u>origin</u> of Trina's family name was uncertain, but it seemed to be
Scandinavian.

Origin means _____.

2 Bradley is proud of his Scottish <u>heritage</u>, so he is learning to play the bagpipes.

Heritage means _____.

3 One of Kiesha's <u>ancestors</u> fought in the American Civil War.

Ancestors means _____.

4 My grandmother is researching her <u>genealogy</u>. She wants to find the first
American in the family.

Genealogy means _____.

5 Black hair and green eyes are part of my <u>heredity</u> from my father's side of
the family.

Heredity means _____.

6 This antique nightstand is my mother's <u>inheritance</u> from her grandmother.

Inheritance means _____.

Context Clues 5

DIRECTIONS **Read each sentence and think about the meaning of the underlined word. Then write a definition of the underlined word.**

1 In dry parts of the country, farmers use irrigation to bring water to their crops.

Irrigation means _____.

2 A canal was built, leading from the lake to the farthest field, to bring water to the crops.

Canal means _____.

3 Farmers must be very knowledgeable about the climate, or weather conditions, in their area.

Climate means _____.

4 We needed a heavy rain to drench the vegetable garden before it dried out completely.

Drench means _____.

5 When the apples are ripe, farmers harvest them and take them to market.

Harvest means _____.

6 If you want to raise crops and farm animals, you should study agriculture in college.

Agriculture means _____.

7 Since the stream had dried up, we kept a trough filled with water for the cows to drink.

Trough means _____.

Context Clues 6

DIRECTIONS Read each sentence or pair of sentences. Think about the meaning of the underlined word. Then write a definition of the underlined word.

1 I <u>strive</u> to do my best at dance class, but I'm still not very good at it.

Strive means _____.

2 Hard work will <u>prevail</u> when all else fails.

Prevail means _____.

3 The cyclist could not <u>endure</u> the heat of the sun and rested until it became cooler.

Endure means _____.

4 We will <u>perpetuate</u> our traffic problems by continuing to buy more cars without expanding the roadways.

Perpetuate means _____.

5 Although learning a new language was difficult, I <u>persevered</u>, and now I can speak Spanish.

Persevered means _____.

6 John's <u>persistence</u> paid off. After hours of searching, he finally found the baseball that his friends had thought was lost.

Persistence means _____.

7 The <u>setting</u> of the story was a desert in the southwestern United States.

Setting means _____.

8 Like a hare, a <u>jackrabbit</u> is a desert-dwelling animal with oversized ears that help it stay cool.

Jackrabbit means _____.

Context Clues 7

DIRECTIONS Read the words in the box. Their meanings are related but not the same. Complete each sentence with the best word from the box.

sequence	arrangement	sequel	continuous
subsequent	organization	order	progression

1 A dictionary lists words in alphabetical _____.

2 A 24-hour television channel offers viewers a _____ broadcast.

3 The ushers seated the guests at the banquet according to the

seating _____.

4 The movie was such a success that the following year the producers made

a _____ to it.

5 Chapter 6 and the _____ chapters in the unit all deal with fractions.

6 We are learning about the _____ of events that led to the Revolutionary War.

7 The _____ of books at the library made it simple for patrons to find what they were looking for.

8 A steady _____ of spectators soon filled the stadium.

DIRECTIONS Now try this. Write a word from the box to complete each phrase.

9 numerical _____

10 _____ progress

11 _____ pages

12 _____ of flowers

Multiple-Meaning Words 1

DIRECTIONS Read each sentence and think about the meaning of the underlined word. Read the definitions of that word. Circle the letter of the meaning used in the sentence.

1 My neighbor is a <u>volunteer</u> at the hospital

   A a person who works without pay

   B to give or offer readily

2 The scientist hopes to <u>engineer</u> a new type of electric motor.

   A a person who builds machines

   B to create and make plans for something

3 The United States of America continues to <u>pioneer</u> space travel.

   A to be the first to do something

   B a person who does something before anyone else

4 The fire <u>chief</u> gives orders to the firefighters.

   A the leader of a group

   B most important, main

5 The team of <u>mountaineers</u> planned to hike in the Himalayas.

   A people who climb or live on a mountain

   B climbs mountains for enjoyment

6 The strong <u>current</u> can pull small boats off their course.

   A present; up to date

   B a stream of water that moves through the ocean

7 Brad found an injured sparrow and will <u>nurse</u> it back to health.

   A a person who takes care of the sick

   B to take care of someone or something that is ill

8 I am learning how to <u>iron</u> my own shirts.

   A to press clothes to remove wrinkles

   B a hard metal

Multiple-Meaning Words 2

DIRECTIONS Read each sentence and think about the meaning of the underlined word. Read the definitions of that word. Circle the letter of the meaning used in the sentence.

1 After the fire all that remained of the old house was a roofless <u>skeleton</u>.

  A the main columns and beams, without walls

  B all the bones of a human body

2 The scientist's years of research laid the <u>framework</u> for his later inventions.

  A the beginning of a house before walls are added

  B a set of ideas from which to begin working

3 They made a pretty dessert by pouring fruit and gelatin into a heart-shaped <u>mold</u>.

  A a pan that gives food a decorative shape

  B a type of fungus found on damp or decaying surfaces

4 Bark and branches are part of the <u>structure</u> of most trees.

  A what something is made of

  B a building

5 The teenager was of a small <u>frame</u> and easily slipped through the railings to save the stranded puppy.

  A an object used for displaying a photograph or painting

  B the physical make-up of the body

6 The tailor uses a <u>form</u> so that his jackets are well-shaped.

  A a model of the upper body used for fitting clothes

  B a document with blank spaces to be filled with information

7 In social studies we are learning about the <u>anatomy</u> of the government.

  A the way that parts are organized

  B the study of the parts of the body

Multiple-Meaning Words 3

DIRECTIONS Read the sentences in each pair. Notice that the same
word is underlined in both sentences. Then read the two definitions
of the underlined word. After each sentence, write the letter of the
definition that is used in that sentence.

1 The smoke from vast forest fires added to the pollution of the

atmosphere. _____

There was an atmosphere of friendly competition when the opposing

teams met for the first time. _____

A the layer of air surrounding the earth

B the surrounding feeling of an environment

2 Citrus trees grow best in a tropical climate. _____

The townspeople couldn't get enough of Yulee's Yummy Yogurt. The

climate was right for Yulee to open a second store. _____

A an atmosphere or feeling among people

B a region having particular weather conditions

3 Ron felt homesick at first, but he soon felt comfortable in his new

surroundings. _____

The trees surrounding the lake were tall and leafy, providing shade

for campers. _____

A enclosing on all sides

B the conditions around you

4 Jerome auditioned for the lead part in the musical. _____

Songbirds and crickets are among the musical animals that live in

the woods. _____

A a dramatic performance that includes singing

B melodious, sounding like music

© Harcourt

Multiple-Meaning Words 4

DIRECTIONS Read each sentence and think about the meaning of the underlined word. Read the definitions of that word. Circle the letter of the meaning used in the sentence.

1 The museum bought a <u>canvas</u> by Vincent van Gogh.

A a painting, often done with oil paints

B a heavy, coarse material

2 I purchased a beautiful <u>landscape</u> for my living-room wall.

A a computer printout with top and bottom being longer than sides

B a picture of natural scenery

3 Porcupines <u>bristle</u> to keep enemies away.

A make quills stand on end

B usually animal hair used in paintbrushes

4 Robert is allergic to wool, so he wears <u>acrylic</u> sweaters.

A a type of water-based paint

B a kind of yarn not made from wool or cotton

5 Helen chose fruit as the <u>subject</u> for her sketches.

A an area of study

B an object represented in art

6 Please <u>chop</u> the onions and the tomatoes.

A to cut with a knife

B a cut of meat

DIRECTIONS Choose two words from the box. Write two meanings for each.

| steer | model | post | yarn | mold |

7 _____   _____

8 _____   _____

Prefixes

All the words in the box begin with the prefix *trans-*, which means "across" or "beyond."

DIRECTIONS Use the words to finish the story below. Choose the best word to use in each blank.

transatlantic	transcontinental	translate	transparent
transmountain	transoceanic	transport	translucent

Josh and Henry decided to travel around the world and visit many countries. They started their world tour in West Africa. They traveled by ship across the Atlantic Ocean. The _____ journey took two weeks. The cabin they stayed in had a _____ window, so although it let sunlight into the room, they could not see the outside.

They docked in New York City, and soon after began their travels across the North American continent. Eventually, they reached San Francisco, on the west coast. Their _____ journey was long but a lot of fun.

They had especially enjoyed their _____ hike across the Rocky Mountains. Once, they stopped at a mountain spring with crystal-clear water. They had never seen such a _____ pool. Josh had wanted to _____ some of the water back home, but they still had far to go.

From California, the men needed to cross the ocean once again, to get to Japan. This time they decided to fly. The _____ journey was much faster by plane than by ship! In Japan, they needed someone to _____ for them in the restaurant. They were very glad to find a waiter who spoke English!

Related Words 1

The words in each group below share the same root, or base word.

DIRECTIONS Read the words in each group and write the base word.

1 expressly, expressionism, expressive _____

2 economist, economics, economically _____

3 settlement, resettlement, settler _____

4 transoceanic, oceanography, oceanfront _____

5 informational, informatively, informant _____

6 marina, mariner, aquamarine _____

7 explainable, explanation, explanatory _____

8 glaciology, glacial, glaciation _____

9 analyst, analyzing, analysis _____

10 geologist, geological, geologic _____

11 mountainous, transmountain, mountaineer _____

12 strategize, strategist, strategic _____

13 competition, competitor, competitive _____

14 sequential, sequentially, sequencing _____

15 relative, relationship, relatedness _____

16 uncooperative, cooperation, cooperator _____

17 urbane, urbanite, suburban _____

18 disinterested, interestingly, uninteresting _____

Related Words 2

The words in each group below share the same root, or base word.

DIRECTIONS Read the words in each group and write the base word.

1 habitat, habitation, inhabit _____

2 humanist, inhuman, humanitarian _____

3 planetary, planetarium, planetoid _____

4 coloration, colorfast, colorist _____

5 viewpoint, interview, review _____

6 interplay, replay, playground _____

7 buildup, rebuild, building _____

8 worker, workplace, overworked _____

9 mistrust, trustworthy, trustful _____

10 nonsense, sensitive, senseless _____

DIRECTIONS Read each word below and read the root from which the word comes. Write another word that has the same root.

11 aquatic   *aqua*   _____

12 subterranean   *terr*   _____

13 temperate   *temp*   _____

14 dictate   *dict*   _____

15 remember   *mem*   _____

© Harcourt

Related Words 3

The words in the groups below are related by roots or base words.

DIRECTIONS Read the words in each group. Circle the letter of the word that is not related to the others. Then write another word that is related to the rest of the group.

1 A demolished
   B demolition
   C demolishing
   D detract

_____

2 A dessert
   B destroy
   C destroyer
   D destroys

_____

3 A devastate
   B vest
   C devastation
   D devastated

_____

4 A obliterates
   B obliteration
   C object
   D obliterating

_____

5 A refurbish
   B refurbishes
   C furniture
   D refurbished

_____

6 A renovate
   B renown
   C renovation
   D renovated

_____

7 A resistance
   B restoration
   C restore
   D restored

_____

8 A revive
   B revived
   C revives
   D revisit

_____

© Harcourt

Related Words 4

The words in the groups below are related by roots or base words.

DIRECTIONS Read the words in each group. Circle the letter of the word that is not related to the others.

1
A irrigate
B irrigation
C irrigating
D irritate

3
A hybrid
B hydrate
C dehydrated
D hydrant

2
A moisten
B moisturize
C moist
D mostly

4
A aqueduct
B aquifer
C acquire
D aquarium

Words can also be related by structural elements such as prefixes, suffixes, or word parts.

DIRECTIONS Circle the letter of the word that is not related to the others in the list. Then write another word that is related to the rest of the group.

5
A runner
B jumping
C throwing
D playing

_____

7
A redo
B reach
C rerun
D reheat

_____

6
A independent
B incorrect
C island
D indirect

_____

8
A ouch
B out-yell
C outdo
D outwalk

_____

Related Words 5

The words in each group below share the same root, or base word.

DIRECTIONS Read the words in each group and write the base word.

1 acculturate, culturist, cultural _____

2 civilization, uncivilized, civility _____

3 society, socialization, antisocial _____

4 befriend, friendliness, friendship _____

5 folktale, folksy, folklore _____

6 misuse, useful, used _____

7 ethnicity, ethnology, multiethnic _____

8 celebration, celebrity, celebrated _____

9 servant, service, serving _____

10 apart, partition, compartment _____

DIRECTIONS Now read each word below. Write two or three words that are related to the base word.

11 joy _____

12 child _____

13 port _____

14 happy _____

15 art _____

16 order _____

Roots 1

The words in the box all come from the Latin root *vita*, which means "life."

DIRECTIONS **Read the words and their definitions. Then complete each sentence below with a word from the box.**

---

revitalize *verb* to give new life or energy to

vitamin *noun* a substance found in food and needed for the body's health and growth

vital *adjective* **1.** necessary to or supporting life **2.** very important or necessary

vitality *noun* **1.** vigor, energy **2.** the capacity to live, grow, and develop

vitalize *verb* **1.** to endow or provide with life **2.** to invigorate or animate

vitals *noun* those bodily organs whose functioning is essential to life

---

1 We get _____ C from eating certain foods.

2 Healthy lungs are _____ to life.

3 Three balanced meals a day help ensure a person's _____.

4 Warm clothing is _____ for a ski vacation.

5 The phrase "full of vim, vigor, and _____" is often used to describe a person who is full of energy.

6 A person's _____ include the brain, the heart, and the lungs.

7 A hearty breakfast will _____ you for the day.

8 When you have been sitting still for a long time, exercise is a great way to

_____ the body.

Roots 2

The Greek root *astro* means "star" or "star-shaped."

DIRECTIONS Use that information to answer the following questions.

1 *Nautical* comes from the Greek word for *sailor*. What does *astronaut* mean?

_____

2 The endings *-ics*, *-ogy*, and *-y* mean "the science or practice of."
What does *astronautics* mean?

_____

What is *astronomy*?

_____

3 The suffix *-er* often means "a person who." What does an *astronomer* do?

_____

4 A *cuboid* is an object shaped something like a cube.
What do you think an *asteroid* is?

_____

5 *Nautical* means "having to do with the sea." What do you think *astral* means?

_____

6 A dome is a rounded roof. What might an *astrodome* be used for?

_____

7 An aster is a type of flower. Draw what you think it might look like.

8 An asterisk is a kind of punctuation mark. Draw what you think it might
look like.

Roots 3

DIRECTIONS Read the Greek roots and their definitions.

Roots	Definitions	Roots	Definitions
auto	self	*photo*	light
bio	life	*tele*	at a distance
graph	written		

DIRECTIONS Write a definition for each word. Use what you already know about the words, as well as the information in the box.

1 biography _____

2 autobiography _____

3 autograph _____

DIRECTIONS Write a word to complete each of the following sentences. Use the Greek roots in the box.

4 A camera uses a special film that is exposed to the light for a very brief moment.

The result is a _____.

5 A pilot is safely in the air and allows the plane to control itself. She puts the

plane on _____.

6 When we watch shows on _____, we see images that are broadcast from a distance.

7 Morse created a machine that sent written messages over a long distance.

It was called a _____, and it used an alphabet called Morse code.

© Harcourt

Roots 4

The Greek root *ped* or *pod* means "foot."

DIRECTIONS Read about the Greek and Latin word parts in the box. Then complete the *ped/pod* web by writing the word that fits each definition.

Word Parts	Definitions	Word Parts	Definitions
cent	hundred	*meter*	measure
ian	one who	*quad*	four
iatry	art of healing	*tri*	three

an instrument for measuring distance walked

_____

an animal with one hundred legs (but not really!)

_____

the healing and treatment of foot problems

_____

ped or *pod*

a three-legged stand often used by photographers

_____

a person who is walking

_____

a base or foot on which to set something

_____

any animal that has four legs

_____

Suffixes 1

Each word in the box ends with the suffix *-eer*, *-er*, or *-or*. These suffixes add the meaning "one who."

DIRECTIONS Use the words from the box to complete the sentences below. Then write a definition of the word you added.

mountaineer	volunteer	photographer
settler	engineer	senator

1 The _____ used a camera with a powerful lens to take pictures of the lions.

_____

2 Long ago, trains used steam engines that were powered by coal.

The train driver was called an _____.

_____

3 As an experienced _____, Joelle planned to climb Mt. McKinley.

_____

4 The voters re-elected the _____ to office because of the work he had done for his state.

_____

DIRECTIONS Write each word defined below. Use words from the box. Then write a sentence using the word.

5 someone who offers to work without receiving payment _____

_____

6 someone who settled in an area before others did _____

_____

Suffixes 2

The suffixes *-er* and *-or* can be added to some verbs to create nouns. These suffixes add the meaning "one who."

DIRECTIONS Write a title for the person who will do each of these jobs in a theater performance. Add a suffix to the underlined verb.

1 <u>choreograph</u> the dance number _____

2 <u>conduct</u> the orchestra _____

3 <u>compose</u> original music for the opening act _____

4 <u>perform</u> in the dance or drama acts _____

DIRECTIONS Think of other people who might participate in a theater performance. Write the verb that tells what each person does. Then add a suffix to create a title for that person.

For example: drum + er = drummer

5 _____ + _____ = _____

6 _____ + _____ = _____

7 _____ + _____ = _____

8 _____ + _____ = _____

DIRECTIONS Write your answers to these questions about words with suffixes.

9 What is the word meaning "one who entertains"? _____

10 Can an *entertainer* be a *volunteer*? Why or why not? _____

_____

Suffixes 3

The suffixes -*tion* and -*ment* can be added to some verbs to create nouns. These suffixes add the meaning "the act of" or "someone or something that."

DIRECTIONS Add the suffix *-tion* or *-ment* to each word below. Then write a definition of the word you made. The first one has been done for you.

1 occupy + tion = ____occupation____

____something that keeps you occupied____

2 communicate + tion = _____

_____

3 educate + tion = _____

_____

4 entertain + ment = _____

_____

5 employ + ment = _____

_____

6 define + tion = _____

_____

7 introduce + tion = _____

_____

8 immigrate + tion = _____

_____

9 inform + tion = _____

_____

10 govern + ment = _____

_____

Suffixes 4

The suffix *-ly* can be added to some words to create adverbs.

DIRECTIONS Read each example and circle the word that ends with the suffix *-ly*. Then answer the question or follow the directions.

1 Wilbur had barely enough time to catch the bus. At right, draw a picture of Wilbur on his way to the bus stop.

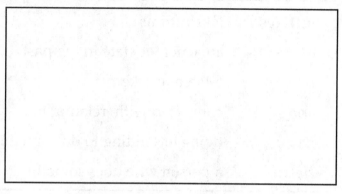

2 Although there was a chill in the air, it was virtually spring.

What season was it? _____

3 Jeb has two quarters, a dime, and three pennies. He wants to buy some apple juice that costs 65 cents. To have precisely the right amount of money, what does Jeb need?

_____

4 The strength of the bridge was measured inaccurately. Explain how you would feel about traveling across it.

_____

5 The park rangers reported seeing approximately 50 deer.

What number could there have been? _____

If they reported nearly 50 deer, how might your answer be different?

_____

6 Brenda has one dollar. Her notebook costs exactly 82 cents.

How much change will she receive? _____

7 The box contains roughly 95 raisins.

What is a synonym for the word you circled? _____

© Harcourt

Suffixes 5

DIRECTIONS Read the suffixes and their definitions. Then complete each sentence below. Add a suffix from the box to the word in parentheses after the sentence.

Suffixes	Definitions
-ed	an action or state in the past
-ic	related to, like
-ary	connected with, relating to
-ive	doing or tending to do something
-er, -ist	a person who does something

1 A _____ is a person who studies the history of the earth. (**geology**)

2 Intense underground heat _____ that rock. (**melt**)

3 The firefighter's actions were _____. (**hero**)

4 The fire _____ all night. (**burn**)

5 The _____ ash fell many miles from the eruption. (**volcano**)

6 Limestone is a _____ rock, formed from small pieces of other rocks. (**sediment**)

7 The museum showed an _____ movie. (**instruct**)

8 A _____ studies the earth and its inhabitants. (**geography**)

Synonyms / Antonyms

Synonyms are words that have the same, or almost the same, meaning.

DIRECTIONS Rewrite each sentence below. Replace the underlined word with a synonym from the box.

weathering	coastline	inquired	simple

1 We <u>asked</u> about the cause of the landslide.

_____

2 Huge waves pounded the <u>shore</u>.

_____

3 If you take your time, the project will be <u>easy</u>.

_____

4 The old cabin showed signs of <u>wear</u>.

_____

Antonyms are words that have opposite, or nearly opposite, meanings.

DIRECTIONS Rewrite each sentence below. Replace the underlined word with an antonym from the box.

erosion	windswept	difficult

5 Harsh winds had resulted in <u>conservation</u> of the soil.

_____

6 We climbed a steep, <u>sheltered</u> cliff.

_____

7 I struggled to answer the <u>easy</u> question.

_____

Synonyms 1

Synonyms are words that have the same, or almost the same, meaning.

DIRECTIONS Complete each web by writing synonyms of the word in the center. Choose your synonyms from the words in the box. One has been done for you.

form	character	mold	expression
identity	look	frame	individuality

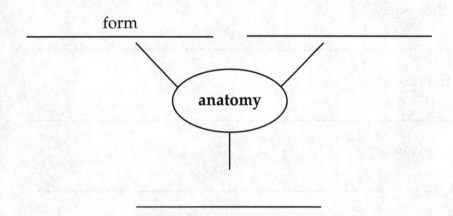

form

anatomy

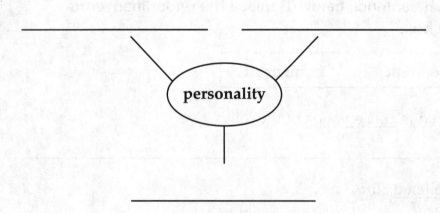

personality

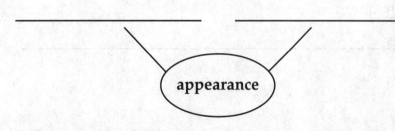

appearance

Synonyms 2

Synonyms are words that have the same, or almost the same, meaning.

DIRECTIONS Complete each web by writing synonyms of the word in the center. Choose your synonyms from the words in the box. One has been done for you.

constant	following	advancement	nonstop	later
uninterrupted		progress	headway	succeeding

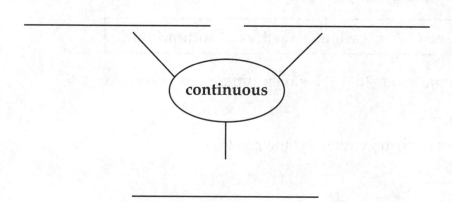

headway

progression

continuous

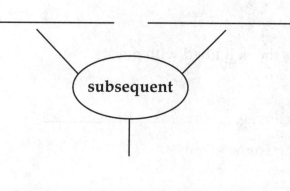

subsequent

© Harcourt

Synonyms 3

Synonyms are words that have the same, or almost the same, meaning.

DIRECTIONS Read the words in the box. Then write each word next to its synonym below.

fortune	approve	damp	occurrence	party	probability

1 likelihood _____

2 humid _____

3 incident _____

4 fiesta _____

5 ratify _____

6 luck _____

DIRECTIONS Read each sentence and think about the meaning of the underlined word. Read the words in the box, and find a synonym of the underlined word. Write the synonym.

chance	dry	country	occasion	settle	auditorium

7 The citizens always found a way to <u>resolve</u> their differences peacefully.

_____

8 Representatives from every <u>nation</u> attended the meeting.

_____

9 The town's one-hundredth anniversary was an important <u>event</u>.

_____

10 There was a lot of excitement as the <u>hall</u> filled with guests.

_____

11 Cactus grows well in that <u>arid</u> climate. _____

12 The <u>likelihood</u> of rain was slight, so the event

was outdoors. _____

Synonyms 4

The words in the box can all be synonyms of *devastate*, but each word has a slightly different meaning.

DIRECTIONS Rewrite each sentence below. Choose the best word to use in place of *devastate*.

harm	spoil	destroy	wreck

1 The dog will not <u>devastate</u> you.

_____

2 A tornado can <u>devastate</u> houses.

_____

3 A raging fire can completely <u>devastate</u> a forest, leaving only ashes.

_____

4 Too much salt will <u>devastate</u> the taste of the soup.

_____

The words in the box can all be synonyms of *rebuild*, but each word has a slightly different meaning.

DIRECTIONS Rewrite each sentence below. Choose the best word to use in place of *rebuild*.

revive	restore	renovate

5 We will <u>rebuild</u> the old house, making it look new.

_____

6 We will clean the painting to <u>rebuild</u> it to its original beauty.

_____

7 These mugs of hot chocolate will <u>rebuild</u> the cold, tired children.

_____

hemisphere	coastal plain
Unit 1, Chapter 1, Lesson 1	Unit 1, Chapter 1, Lesson 2
equator	harbor
Unit 1, Chapter 1, Lesson 1	Unit 1, Chapter 1, Lesson 2
prime meridian	tributary
Unit 1, Chapter 1, Lesson 1	Unit 1, Chapter 1, Lesson 2
relative location	delta
Unit 1, Chapter 1, Lesson 1	Unit 1, Chapter 1, Lesson 2
natural region	fertile
Unit 1, Chapter 1, Lesson 2	Unit 1, Chapter 1, Lesson 2

© Harcourt

An area of low land that lies along the shoreline.	A half of Earth.
A protected area of water where ships can dock safely.	The imaginary line that divides Earth into the Northern Hemisphere and the Southern Hemisphere.
A river that flows into a larger river.	The imaginary line that divides Earth into the Western Hemisphere and the Eastern Hemisphere.
Land built up from soil carried by rivers.	Where a place is in relation to one or more other places on Earth.
Good for growing crops.	A region made up of places that share the same kinds of physical, or natural, features, such as plains, mountains, valleys, or deserts.

irrigation	humid
Unit 1, Chapter 1, Lesson 2	Unit 1, Chapter 1, Lesson 3
sea level	rain shadow
Unit 1, Chapter 1, Lesson 2	Unit 1, Chapter 1, Lesson 3
precipitation	drought
Unit 1, Chapter 1, Lesson 3	Unit 1, Chapter 1, Lesson 3
climate	physical environment
Unit 1, Chapter 1, Lesson 3	Unit 1, Chapter 1, Lesson 4
vegetation	natural resource
Unit 1, Chapter 1, Lesson 3	Unit 1, Chapter 1, Lesson 4

© Harcourt

Damp or moist.	The use of canals, ditches, or pipes to carry water to dry places.
The drier side of a mountain.	The level of the surface of the ocean.
A long time with little or no rain.	Water that falls to Earth's surface as rain, sleet, hail, or snow.
Surroundings consisting of a place's physical features, landforms, and climate.	The kind of weather a place has most often, year after year.
Something found in nature, such as water, soil, or minerals, that people can use to meet their needs.	Plant life.

urban Unit 1, Chapter 1, Lesson 4	**adapt** Unit 1, Chapter 1, Lesson 5
metropolitan area Unit 1, Chapter 1, Lesson 4	**service** Unit 1, Chapter 1, Lesson 5
suburb Unit 1, Chapter 1, Lesson 4	**industry** Unit 1, Chapter 1, Lesson 5
rural Unit 1, Chapter 1, Lesson 4	**fault** Unit 1, Chapter 1, Lesson 5
modify Unit 1, Chapter 1, Lesson 4	**growing season** Unit 1, Chapter 1, Lesson 5

To change one's way of life to adjust to the environment.	Like, in, or of a city.
An activity that someone does for others for pay.	A large city together with nearby cities and suburbs.
All the businesses that make one kind of product or provide one kind of service.	A town or small city near a large city.
A crack in Earth's surface.	Like, in, or of the country.
The period of time when the weather is warm enough for crops to grow.	To change.

scarce

Unit 1, Chapter 1, Lesson 5

Limited.

glacier	artifact
Unit 1, Chapter 2, Lesson 1	Unit 1, Chapter 2, Lesson 1
ancestor	legend
Unit 1, Chapter 2, Lesson 1	Unit 1, Chapter 2, Lesson 1
surplus	weir
Unit 1, Chapter 2, Lesson 1	Unit 1, Chapter 2, Lesson 2
tribe	ceremony
Unit 1, Chapter 2, Lesson 1	Unit 1, Chapter 2, Lesson 2
culture	shaman
Unit 1, Chapter 2, Lesson 1	Unit 1, Chapter 2, Lesson 2

© Harcourt

Any object made by people in the past.	A huge, slow-moving mass of ice.
A story handed down over time.	An early family member.
A fence-like structure built across a river in order to trap fish.	An extra amount.
A celebration to honor a cultural or religious event.	An American Indian group with its own leaders and lands.
A religious leader.	A way of life.

trade	specialize
Unit 1, Chapter 2, Lesson 2	Unit 1, Chapter 2, Lesson 4
government	spring
Unit 1, Chapter 2, Lesson 3	Unit 1, Chapter 2, Lesson 5
cooperate	arid
Unit 1, Chapter 2, Lesson 3	Unit 1, Chapter 2, Lesson 5
granary	silt
Unit 1, Chapter 2, Lesson 4	Unit 1, Chapter 2, Lesson 5
division of labor	agriculture
Unit 1, Chapter 2, Lesson 4	Unit 1, Chapter 2, Lesson 5

© Harcourt

To work at one kind of job and learn to do it well.	The exchanging, or buying and selling, of goods.
A flow of water from an opening in the ground.	A system for deciding what is best for a group of people.
Dry, or having little rainfall.	To work together.
Fine grains of soil and rock.	A place for storing acorns and grains.
Farming.	Having different workers do different jobs.

conquistador Unit 2, Chapter 3, Lesson 1	**ocean current** Unit 2, Chapter 3, Lesson 1
cost Unit 2, Chapter 3, Lesson 1	**wind pattern** Unit 2, Chapter 3, Lesson 1
benefit Unit 2, Chapter 3, Lesson 1	**colony** Unit 2, Chapter 3, Lesson 2
peninsula Unit 2, Chapter 3, Lesson 1	**mission** Unit 2, Chapter 3, Lesson 2
galleon Unit 2, Chapter 3, Lesson 1	**missionary** Unit 2, Chapter 3, Lesson 2

A stream of water that moves through the ocean.	Any of the Spanish conquerors in the Americas.
The general direction of the wind.	The value of something given up in order to gain something.
A settlement that is ruled by a faraway government.	Something that is helpful or gained.
A religious settlement.	Land that has water almost all around it.
A person who teaches a religion to others.	A large Spanish trading ship.

expedition Unit 2, Chapter 3, Lesson 2	**economy** Unit 2, Chapter 3, Lesson 4
presidio Unit 2, Chapter 3, Lesson 3	**neophyte** Unit 2, Chapter 3, Lesson 4
pueblo Unit 2, Chapter 3, Lesson 3	**revolt** Unit 2, Chapter 3, Lesson 4
plaza Unit 2, Chapter 3, Lesson 3	**custom** Unit 2, Chapter 3, Lesson 4
alcalde Unit 2, Chapter 3, Lesson 3	

The way people in a place or region use resources to meet their needs.	A journey into an area to learn more about it.
A person who is new to the Catholic faith.	A Spanish fort.
To fight against.	A farming community in Spanish California.
A usual way of doing things.	An open square where people can gather.
	A mayor of a town in Spanish California.

independence	land grant
Unit 2, Chapter 4, Lesson 1	Unit 2, Chapter 4, Lesson 2
criollo	diseño
Unit 2, Chapter 4, Lesson 1	Unit 2, Chapter 4, Lesson 2
mestizo	rancho
Unit 2, Chapter 4, Lesson 1	Unit 2, Chapter 4, Lesson 2
Californio	hacienda
Unit 2, Chapter 4, Lesson 1	Unit 2, Chapter 4, Lesson 2
secularization	barter
Unit 2, Chapter 4, Lesson 1	Unit 2, Chapter 4, Lesson 2

© Harcourt

A gift of land given by the government.	Freedom.
A hand-drawn map that shows the boundaries of a land grant.	A person born of Spanish parents in Mexico.
A cattle ranch.	A person of both European and Indian heritage who lived in Mexico or another part of New Spain.
The main house on a rancho.	The name that the Spanish-speaking people of Alta California called themselves.
To trade one kind of item for another, usually without exchanging money.	The end of church rule of the missions.

tallow

Unit 2, Chapter 4, Lesson 2

vaquero

Unit 2, Chapter 4, Lesson 3

labor

Unit 2, Chapter 4, Lesson 3

fiesta

Unit 2, Chapter 4, Lesson 3

© Harcourt

	Animal fat used to make soap and candles.
	A cowhand.
	Work.
	A party.

© Harcourt

demand Unit 3, Chapter 5, Lesson 1	**immigrant** Unit 3, Chapter 5, Lesson 2
supply Unit 3, Chapter 5, Lesson 1	**pioneer** Unit 3, Chapter 5, Lesson 2
frontier Unit 3, Chapter 5, Lesson 1	**wagon train** Unit 3, Chapter 5, Lesson 2
trailblazer Unit 3, Chapter 5, Lesson 1	**manifest destiny** Unit 3, Chapter 5, Lesson 3
pass Unit 3, Chapter 5, Lesson 1	**squatter** Unit 3, Chapter 5, Lesson 3

A person who comes from another place to live in a country.	A need or a desire for a good or service by people willing to pay for it.
One of the first settlers in a place.	An amount of a good or a service that is offered for sale.
A group of wagons, each pulled by horses or oxen.	Land beyond the settled part of a country.
The idea that the United States should expand to reach from the Atlantic Ocean to the Pacific Ocean.	A person who makes a new trail for others to follow.
Someone who lives in a place without permission.	An opening between high mountains.

© Harcourt

rebel

Unit 3, Chapter 5, Lesson 3

republic

Unit 3, Chapter 5, Lesson 3

right

Unit 3, Chapter 5, Lesson 4

treaty

Unit 3, Chapter 5, Lesson 4

	A person who fights against the government.
	A form of government in which people elect their leaders.
	A freedom that belongs to a person.
	A written agreement between groups or countries.

gold rush	entrepreneur
Unit 3, Chapter 6, Lesson 1	Unit 3, Chapter 6, Lesson 2
forty-niner	inflation
Unit 3, Chapter 6, Lesson 1	Unit 3, Chapter 6, Lesson 2
isthmus	discrimination
Unit 3, Chapter 6, Lesson 1	Unit 3, Chapter 6, Lesson 2
claim	vigilante
Unit 3, Chapter 6, Lesson 1	Unit 3, Chapter 6, Lesson 2
consumer	convention
Unit 3, Chapter 6, Lesson 2	Unit 3, Chapter 6, Lesson 3

A person who sets up a new business.	A huge movement of people going to a place to look for gold.
A sharp increase in prices.	A person who went to California in 1849 to search for gold.
The unfair treatment of people because of such things as their religion, their race, or their birthplace.	A narrow piece of land that connects two larger land areas.
A person who takes the law into his or her own hands.	The area a miner said belonged to him or her.
An important meeting.	A person who buys a product or a service.

delegate	compromise
Unit 3, Chapter 6, Lesson 3	Unit 3, Chapter 6, Lesson 3
constitution	
Unit 3, Chapter 6, Lesson 3	
legislature	
Unit 3, Chapter 6, Lesson 3	
ratify	
Unit 3, Chapter 6, Lesson 3	
Congress	
Unit 3, Chapter 6, Lesson 3	

© Harcourt

An agreement in which each side in a conflict gives up some of what it wants.	A person who is chosen to speak and act for the people who elected him or her.
	A plan of government.
	A group of officials elected to make laws.
	To approve.
	The part of the United States government that makes laws.

communication Unit 4, Chapter 7, Lesson 1	**competition** Unit 4, Chapter 7, Lesson 3
stagecoach Unit 4, Chapter 7, Lesson 1	**commercial farm** Unit 4, Chapter 7, Lesson 4
telegraph Unit 4, Chapter 7, Lesson 1	**export** Unit 4, Chapter 7, Lesson 4
transcontinental railroad Unit 4, Chapter 7, Lesson 2	**tenant farmer** Unit 4, Chapter 7, Lesson 4
invest Unit 4, Chapter 7, Lesson 2	**canal** Unit 4, Chapter 7, Lesson 4

The contest among companies to get the most customers or sell the most products.	The sending and receiving of information.
A farm that grows crops only to sell.	An enclosed wagon pulled by a team of horses.
A product shipped from one country to be sold in another; to sell goods to people in another country.	A machine that uses electricity to send messages over wires.
A farmer who pays rent to use a piece of land.	A railroad that crosses the North American continent, linking the Atlantic and Pacific coasts.
A waterway dug across land.	To buy something, such as a share in a company, in the hope that it will be worth more in the future.

levee

Unit 4, Chapter 7, Lesson 4

A high wall made of earth to
help control flooding.

immigration Unit 4, Chapter 8, Lesson 1	**boom** Unit 4, Chapter 8, Lesson 2
migration Unit 4, Chapter 8, Lesson 1	**derrick** Unit 4, Chapter 8, Lesson 2
prejudice Unit 4, Chapter 8, Lesson 1	**reservoir** Unit 4, Chapter 8, Lesson 2
reservation Unit 4, Chapter 8, Lesson 1	**aqueduct** Unit 4, Chapter 8, Lesson 2
petroleum Unit 4, Chapter 8, Lesson 2	**hydroelectric power** Unit 4, Chapter 8, Lesson 2

A time of fast economic growth.	The process of people leaving one country to live in another.
A tower built over an oil well to hold the machines used for drilling.	The movement of people from one place to another within a country.
A lake made by people to collect and store water.	The unfair feeling of hate or dislike for members of a certain group because of their background, race, or religion.
A large pipe or canal that carries water from one place to another.	Land set aside by the government for use by American Indians.
Electricity produced by using waterpower.	Another name for oil.

naturalist

Unit 4, Chapter 8, Lesson 3

A person who studies nature
and works to protect it.

bribe Unit 5, Chapter 9, Lesson 1	**aviation** Unit 5, Chapter 9, Lesson 1
reform Unit 5, Chapter 9, Lesson 1	**stock** Unit 5, Chapter 9, Lesson 2
amendment Unit 5, Chapter 9, Lesson 1	**depression** Unit 5, Chapter 9, Lesson 2
suffrage Unit 5, Chapter 9, Lesson 1	**unemployment** Unit 5, Chapter 9, Lesson 2
consumer good Unit 5, Chapter 9, Lesson 1	**migrant worker** Unit 5, Chapter 9, Lesson 2

The making and flying of airplanes.	To promise money or a gift to a person to get him or her to do something.
A share of ownership in a company.	To change for the better.
A time when there are few jobs and people have little money.	An addition or change to a constitution.
The number of workers without jobs.	The right to vote.
A worker who moves from place to place, harvesting crops.	A product made for people to use.

© Harcourt

munitions

Unit 5, Chapter 9, Lesson 3

shortage

Unit 5, Chapter 9, Lesson 3

bracero

Unit 5, Chapter 9, Lesson 3

recycle

Unit 5, Chapter 9, Lesson 3

relocation camp

Unit 5, Chapter 9, Lesson 3

	Military supplies and weapons.
	A lack of something.
	A skilled Mexican worker who came to California to work during World War II.
	To use again.
	A prison-like camp where Japanese Americans were sent after the bombing of Pearl Harbor.

diverse economy Unit 5, Chapter 10, Lesson 1	**high-tech** Unit 5, Chapter 10, Lesson 1
technology Unit 5, Chapter 10, Lesson 1	**silicon chip** Unit 5, Chapter 10, Lesson 1
freeway Unit 5, Chapter 10, Lesson 1	**aerospace** Unit 5, Chapter 10, Lesson 1
commute Unit 5, Chapter 10, Lesson 1	**segregation** Unit 5, Chapter 10, Lesson 2
urban sprawl Unit 5, Chapter 10, Lesson 1	**civil rights** Unit 5, Chapter 10, Lesson 2

Shortened form of the words *high technology*; having to do with inventing, building, or using computers and other kinds of electronic equipment.	An economy that is based on many industries.
A tiny device that can store millions of bits of information.	The use of knowledge or tools to make or do something.
Having to do with building and testing equipment for air and space travel.	A wide, divided highway with no cross streets or stoplights.
Keeping people of one race or culture separate from other people.	To travel back and forth between work and home.
The rights of citizens to equal treatment.	The outward spread of urban areas.

labor union Unit 5, Chapter 10, Lesson 2	**heritage** Unit 5, Chapter 10, Lesson 3
strike Unit 5, Chapter 10, Lesson 2	
boycott Unit 5, Chapter 10, Lesson 2	
multicultural Unit 5, Chapter 10, Lesson 3	
ethnic group Unit 5, Chapter 10, Lesson 3	

Traditions, beliefs, and ways of life that have been handed down from the past.	An organization of workers whose goal is to improve working conditions.
	A time when workers stop working to get employers to listen to their needs.
	A decision by a group of people not to buy something until a certain problem is fixed.
	Having many different cultures.
	A group of people from the same country, of the same race, or with a shared culture.

international trade Unit 6, Chapter 11, Lesson 1	**tourism** Unit 6, Chapter 11, Lesson 1
import Unit 6, Chapter 11, Lesson 1	**special effect** Unit 6, Chapter 11, Lesson 2
interdependence Unit 6, Chapter 11, Lesson 1	**public school** Unit 6, Chapter 11, Lesson 3
food processing Unit 6, Chapter 11, Lesson 1	**private school** Unit 6, Chapter 11, Lesson 3
service industry Unit 6, Chapter 11, Lesson 1	**generation** Unit 6, Chapter 11, Lesson 3

© Harcourt

The business of serving visitors.	Trade with other countries.
A way of making things that are not real look real on film.	A good, or product, that is brought into one country from another to be sold; to bring in goods from another country to sell.
A school that is free to students, supported by tax dollars, and run by a government agency.	The depending on one another for resources and products.
A school that is funded and run by individuals or groups instead of by a government agency.	The cooking, canning, drying, freezing, and preparing of foods for market.
A group of people born and living at about the same time.	Businesses that do things for people instead of making things.

energy crisis Unit 6, Chapter 11, Lesson 4	**pollution** Unit 6, Chapter 11, Lesson 4
long-term planning Unit 6, Chapter 11, Lesson 4	**deficit** Unit 6, Chapter 11, Lesson 4
conservation Unit 6, Chapter 11, Lesson 4	
renewable Unit 6, Chapter 11, Lesson 4	
nonrenewable Unit 6, Chapter 11, Lesson 4	

Anything that makes a natural resource dirty or unsafe to use.	A problem that happens when there is not enough power to meet demand.
The result of spending more money than is available.	Making choices that are based on how they will affect life in the future.
	The protection and wise use of natural resources.
	Something that can be made again by nature or by people.
	Something that cannot be made again by nature or by people.

democracy Unit 6, Chapter 12, Lesson 1	**budget** Unit 6, Chapter 12, Lesson 2
federal Unit 6, Chapter 12, Lesson 1	**veto** Unit 6, Chapter 12, Lesson 2
Cabinet Unit 6, Chapter 12, Lesson 1	**recall** Unit 6, Chapter 12, Lesson 2
tax Unit 6, Chapter 12, Lesson 1	**initiative** Unit 6, Chapter 12, Lesson 2
bill Unit 6, Chapter 12, Lesson 2	**petition** Unit 6, Chapter 12, Lesson 2

A written plan for how to spend money.	A form of government in which the people rule by making decisions themselves or by electing people to make decisions for them.
To reject.	National.
To remove an official from his or her job.	A group of the President's most important advisers.
A law made directly by voters instead of by a legislature.	Money that a government collects from its citizens, often to pay for services.
A signed request for action.	A plan for a new law.

referendum Unit 6, Chapter 12, Lesson 2	**municipal** Unit 6, Chapter 12, Lesson 3
county Unit 6, Chapter 12, Lesson 3	**city manager** Unit 6, Chapter 12, Lesson 3
county seat Unit 6, Chapter 12, Lesson 3	**special district** Unit 6, Chapter 12, Lesson 3
board of supervisors Unit 6, Chapter 12, Lesson 3	**regional body** Unit 6, Chapter 12, Lesson 3
jury trial Unit 6, Chapter 12, Lesson 3	**rancheria** Unit 6, Chapter 12, Lesson 3

Having to do with a city.	An election in which voters can decide whether to keep or do away with an existing law.
A person hired by a city council to run the city under the direction of a city council.	A section of a state.
A group set up to deal with a certain service or problem.	A city where the main government offices of the county are located.
A group made up of people, usually from several cities or counties, who work together to create a plan for a large area.	An elected group of people who govern a county.
Land in California set aside for American Indians.	A trial in which a group of citizens decides whether a person accused of a crime or other wrongdoing should be found guilty or not guilty.

sovereign

Unit 6, Chapter 12, Lesson 3

	Free and independent.

Answer Key

Antonyms 1 (p. 14)
1. non/nonfiction
2. un/unrealistic
3. un/unnatural
4. non/nonflammable

5–8. Pictures will vary. Students' drawings should illustrate the different meanings of the two antonyms in each pair.

Antonyms 2 (p. 15)
1. professional/amateur
2. fatigue/energy
3. dabbler/expert
4. exports/imports
5. veteran/rookie
6. benefit/disadvantage
7. trainee/trainer

Compound Words (p. 16)
Compound words will vary. Possible words are given.
1. armrest
2. download
3. skyline
4. waterfall
5. self-defense
6. football
7. landmark
8. tablecloth
9. doorknob
10. playground
11. toothbrush
12. overhead
13. underground
14. supermarket
15. anywhere
16. springtime

Content-Area Words 1 (p. 17)
1. ancestor
2. heritage/inheritance/heredity
3. genealogy
4. origin
5. history
6. legacy/inheritance
7. ancestor
8. history
9. genealogy

Content-Area Words 2 (p. 18)
1. marine/nautical/maritime/naval/ mariner/oceanic/submarine
2. coastal
3. marine/maritime/mariner/submarine
4. nautical/naval
5. submarine
6. mariner
7. marine/maritime/naval
8. nautical/naval

Possible word: navy

Content-Area Words 3 (p. 19)
1. irrigate/moisten/hydrate/drench
2. irrigate
3. moisten
4. drench
5. trough/canal/aqueduct/sluice
6. sluice
7. canal
8. Words will vary. Possible words: ocean/lake/ pool/pond/river/stream/creek/inlet/rain

Content-Area Words 4 (p. 20)
1. anatomy
2. drama
3. social studies
4. music
5. grammar
6. mathematics
7. art
8. sports
9. architecture
10. language arts

Labels and additional words will vary. Possible responses are given.

social studies: borders, natural resources, economy, region

sports: baseball, golf, tennis, skating

Content-Area Words 5 (p. 21)
1. civilization/culture/society/ethnicity
2. arts/Examples will vary.
   Possible example: dance
3. language/Other words will vary.
   Possible words: signs, gestures
4. folklore/Examples will vary.
   Possible example: the story of Paul Bunyan
5. cuisine/Dishes will vary.
   Possible dishes: tacos, enchiladas, mole sauce

Content-Area Words 6 (p. 22)

Words will vary. Possible words are given.

Language
    Spanish/English/Arabic/Chinese
Arts
    dance/painting/sculpture/music
Cuisine
    fried rice/sushi/tamales/sauerkraut
Folklore
    myths/fairy tales/legends/tall tales

Content-Area Words 7 (p. 23)

1. habitat

Added inhabitants will vary. Possible responses are given.

2. aquatic/dolphins
3. tropical/frogs
4. arid/coyote
5. subterranean/gophers
6. arctic/penguins
7. temperate/oak trees
8. alpine/mountain lions

Content-Area Words 8 (p. 24)

[left side of web, top to bottom]
    valley
    source
    oasis
    inlet
[right side of web, top to bottom]
    tributary
    meander
    delta
    tidal

Content-Area Words 9 (p. 25)

Added words will vary. Possible words are given.
Words Related to Artist's Tools
    easel/acrylic/bristle/palette/brush
Words Related to Both
    canvas/oil paint
Words Related to a Piece of Art
    subject/landscape/impression/portrait

Content-Area Words 10 (p. 26)

urban: boulevard, skyscraper, downtown, city center, subway, civic, municipal, metropolitan, commerce; rural: lane, ranch, agriculture
Likenesses
    boulevard/lane/downtown/commerce
Differences: Urban
    skyscraper/city center/subway/civic/
    metropolitan
Differences: Rural
    ranch/municipal/agriculture

Content-Area Words 11 (p. 27)

1. news story/records you keep about your own life
2. novel/kinds of poems
3. magazine/parts of a computer
4. movie/things you read
5. computer/things you use to write by hand
6. reply/things you use for writing and sending a letter
7. reader/people who make books
8. plot/physical parts of a book

Content-Area Words 12 (p. 28)

Marine Resources
    minerals/oil/gas
Coastal Features
    dunes/beach/bay
Names
    Atlantic/Pacific/Arctic
Marine Life
    lobsters/oysters/seaweed

Content-Area Words 13 (p. 29)

1. literature
2. fable
3. nonfiction
4. folktale
5. fiction
6. poetry
7. narrative
8. myth

Titles and genres will vary. Possible response: *Where the Sidewalk Ends*, poetry

Content-Area Words 14 (p. 30)

1. pedestal
2. plaque
3. monument
4. dedication
5. sculpt
6. scaffold
7. pedestrian

Students' drawings should show scaffolding and a pedestrian.

Content-Area Words 15 (p. 31)

1. auditory/ocular/olfactory
2. nocturnal/diurnal
3. extraordinary
4. extra-sensitive
5. perception
6. auditory
7. ocular
8. olfactory

© Harcourt

Content-Area Words 16 (p. 32)

Synonyms
    wear/abrasion
Causes
    glacier/weather
Words That Name Affected Places
    coastline/gravel
Words That Describe Affected Areas
    barren/windswept

Context Clues 1 (p. 33)

1. C   money earned by a business
2. C   supplies
3. D   a plan for saving and spending
4. B   sharing information
5. A   a venture to earn a living

Context Clues 2 (p. 34)

1. A   of great importance
2. C   lacking the necessary amount
3. B   something in addition to
4. B   bodily strength
5. D   renewed in energy or liveliness

Context Clues 3 (p. 35)

1. a place where rare trees and shrubs are grown
2. the study of plants
3. a person who studies plants
4. plants
5. a building where delicate plants grow
6. a place where flowers and vegetables grow
7. plant growth
8. related to the study of plants
9. produce flowers

Context Clues 4 (p. 36)

1. place where something began
2. something that comes to you by birth
3. relatives who lived long ago
4. record of events in a family over a long time
5. traits passed down from parents to their children
6. things handed down from a previous generation

Context Clues 5 (p. 37)

1. the use of canals, ditches, or pipes to carry water to dry places
2. a waterway dug across land
3. weather conditions
4. soak
5. pick
6. farming
7. a container of water for animals

Context Clues 6 (p. 38)

1. try hard
2. succeed
3. put up with
4. keep something going
5. kept trying
6. continued effort
7. place a story happens
8. a kind of rabbit that lives in the desert

Context Clues 7 (p. 39)

1. order
2. continuous
3. arrangement
4. sequel
5. subsequent
6. sequence
7. organization
8. progression
Phrases may vary.
9. sequence
10. continuous
11. subsequent
12. arrangement

Multiple-Meaning Words 1 (p. 40)

1. A   a person who works without pay
2. B   to create and make plans for something
3. A   to be the first to do something
4. A   the leader of a group
5. A   people who climb or live on a mountain
6. B   a stream of water that moves through the ocean
7. B   to take care of someone or something that is ill
8. A   to press clothes to remove wrinkles

Multiple-Meaning Words 2 (p. 41)

1. A   the main columns and beams, without walls
2. B   a set of ideas from which to begin working
3. A   a pan that gives food a decorative shape
4. A   what something is made of
5. B   the physical make-up of the body
6. A   a model of the upper body used for fitting clothes
7. A   the way that parts are organized

Multiple-Meaning Words 3 (p. 42)

1. A the layer of air surrounding the earth
   B the surrounding feeling of an environment
2. B a region having particular weather conditions
   A an atmosphere or feeling among people
3. B the conditions around you
   A enclosing on all sides
4. A a dramatic performance that includes singing
   B melodious, sounding like music

Multiple-Meaning Words 4 (p. 43)

1. A a painting, often done with oil paints
2. B a picture of natural scenery
3. A make quills stand on end
4. B a kind of yarn not made from wool or cotton
5. B an object represented in art
6. A to cut with a knife

Words and meanings will vary. Possible responses are given.

7. model: an example worth imitating
   model: a person who poses for photographers
8. post: to put up on a wall
   post: a job or duty

Prefixes (p. 44)

transatlantic
translucent
transcontinental
transmountain
transparent
transport
transoceanic
translate

Related Words 1 (p. 45)

1. express
2. economy
3. settle
4. ocean
5. inform
6. marine
7. explain
8. glacier
9. analyze
10. geology
11. mountain
12. strategy
13. compete
14. sequence
15. relate
16. cooperate
17. urban
18. interest

Related Words 2 (p. 46)

1. habit
2. human
3. planet
4. color
5. view
6. play
7. build
8. work
9. trust
10. sense

Words will vary. Possible words are given.

11. aquarium
12. terrarium
13. temperature
14. dictionary
15. memory

Related Words 3 (p. 47)

Added words will vary. Possible words are given.

1. D detract/demolisher
2. A dessert/destruction
3. B vest/devastating
4. C object/obliterated
5. C furniture/refurbishing
6. B renown/renovating
7. A resistance/restoring
8. D revisit/revival

Related Words 4 (p. 48)

1. D irritate
2. D mostly
3. A hybrid
4. C acquire

Added words will vary. Possible words are given.

5. A runner/skipping
6. C island/incomplete
7. B reach/replay
8. A ouch/outrun

Related Words 5 (p. 49)

1. culture
2. civil
3. social
4. friend
5. folk
6. use
7. ethnic
8. celebrate
9. serve
10. part

Related words will vary. Possible words are given.

11. joyful, enjoy, enjoyable
12. childish, childlike, childhood
13. export, import
14. unhappy, happiness
15. artist, artistic, artful
16. reorder, preorder

Roots 1 (p. 50)

1. vitamin
2. vital
3. vitality
4. vital
5. vitality
6. vitals
7. vitalize
8. revitalize

Roots 2 (p. 51)

1. sailor among the stars
2. the science of space flight/the science of stars
3. studies stars
4. something shaped like a star
5. having to do with stars
6. looking at stars
7. Students' drawings should show star-shaped flowers.
8. Students' drawings should show star-shaped punctuation marks (*).

Roots 3 (p. 52)

1. the written story of someone's life
2. the written story of the writer's own life
3. your own handwritten name
4. photograph
5. autopilot
6. television
7. telegraph

Roots 4 (p. 53)

[starting from top, then left to right]
pedometer
centipede
podiatry
tripod
pedestrian
pedestal
quadruped

Suffixes 1 (p. 54)

1. photographer/one who takes photographs
2. engineer/one who drives an engine
3. mountaineer/one who climbs mountains
4. senator/one who serves in the senate
5. volunteer/Sentences will vary.
   Possible sentence: The coaches of some other teams are paid, but our coach is a volunteer.

6. settler/Sentences will vary.
   Possible sentence: The settler built a small cabin at the edge of the woods.

Suffixes 2 (p. 55)

1. choreographer
2. conductor
3. composer
4. performer

Verbs and titles will vary. Possible responses are given.

5. dance + er = dancer
6. direct + or = director
7. play + er = player
8. help + er = helper
9. entertainer
10. Yes, an entertainer might be a volunteer if he or she is not paid for entertaining.

Suffixes 3 (p. 56)

1. occupation/something that keeps you occupied
2. communication/the act of communicating
3. education/something that educates you
4. entertainment/something that entertains you
5. employment/something that employs you
6. definition/something that defines a word or other thing
7. introduction/the act of introducing
8. immigration/the act of immigrating
9. information/something that informs you
10. government/the act of governing

Suffixes 4 (p. 57)

1. barely/Drawings will vary.
   Students' drawings should show a boy or man rushing.
2. virtually/winter
3. precisely/two more pennies
4. inaccurately/unsafe
5. approximately/There could have been 48 deer, 53 deer, or another number close to 50./ nearly/It would be a number slightly less than 50.
6. exactly/18 cents
7. roughly/approximately

Suffixes 5 (p. 58)

1. geologist
2. melted
3. heroic
4. burned
5. volcanic
6. sedimentary
7. instructive
8. geographer

Synonyms/Antonyms (p. 59)

1. We inquired about the cause of the landslide.
2. Huge waves pounded the coastline.
3. If you take your time, the project will be simple.
4. The old cabin showed signs of weathering.
5. Harsh winds had resulted in erosion of the soil.
6. We climbed a steep, windswept cliff.
7. I struggled to answer the difficult question.

Synonyms 1 (p. 60)

anatomy: form/mold/frame
personality: character/identity/individuality
appearance: look/expression

Synonyms 2 (p. 61)

progression: headway/advancement/progress
continuous: constant/nonstop/uninterrupted
subsequent: following/later/succeeding

Synonyms 3 (p. 62)

1. probability
2. damp
3. occurrence
4. party
5. approve
6. fortune
7. settle
8. country
9. occasion
10. auditorium
11. dry
12. chance

Synonyms 4 (p. 63)

1. The dog will not harm you.
2. A tornado can wreck houses.
3. A raging fire can completely destroy a forest, leaving only ashes.
4. Too much salt will spoil the taste of the soup.
5. We will renovate the old house, making it look new.
6. We will clean the painting to restore it to its original beauty.
7. These mugs of hot chocolate will revive the cold, tired children.